The Big Girl Color Book
MOUNT SHASTA OF THE CASCADE RANGE
Magic, Mystery and Majesty

I0439361

In 2014 I created an artwork "Mt. Shasta with Taiko" and submitted it to the Siskiyou County Fair as a mixed media piece. It won best of show in it's category. My friend Michael, who was badly injured, saw a copy of that picture and said it made him feel like getting well enough to climb on Mount Shasta again. I said I would try do more of the same type of picture and post them to make him feel better. I even had a little art show when he finally came home.

I had so much fun doing these I thought others might like to try coloring my mountain sketches too!

W. Welbourn – Mount Shasta

I dedicate this color book to Carrie, Alison and Paul

These twelve sketches are from photographs I have taken over the years here in Siskiyou County. Oh, and my imagination! Please see tiny versions of my photos on the back cover of this book.

CONTENTS   (The coloring pages are in horizontal layout)

Find a comfortable, quiet spot where you can spend some time. Use colored pencils. If you use wet markers, consider removing the page from the book and working on a blotter. There is a blank page at the end of this book that can be removed and used as a blotter between pages.

As you color, enjoy the magic that Mount Shasta created for me.

If you need inspiration please see my blog:
www.TBGCB.blogspot.com
This Google blog uses cookies to track visits

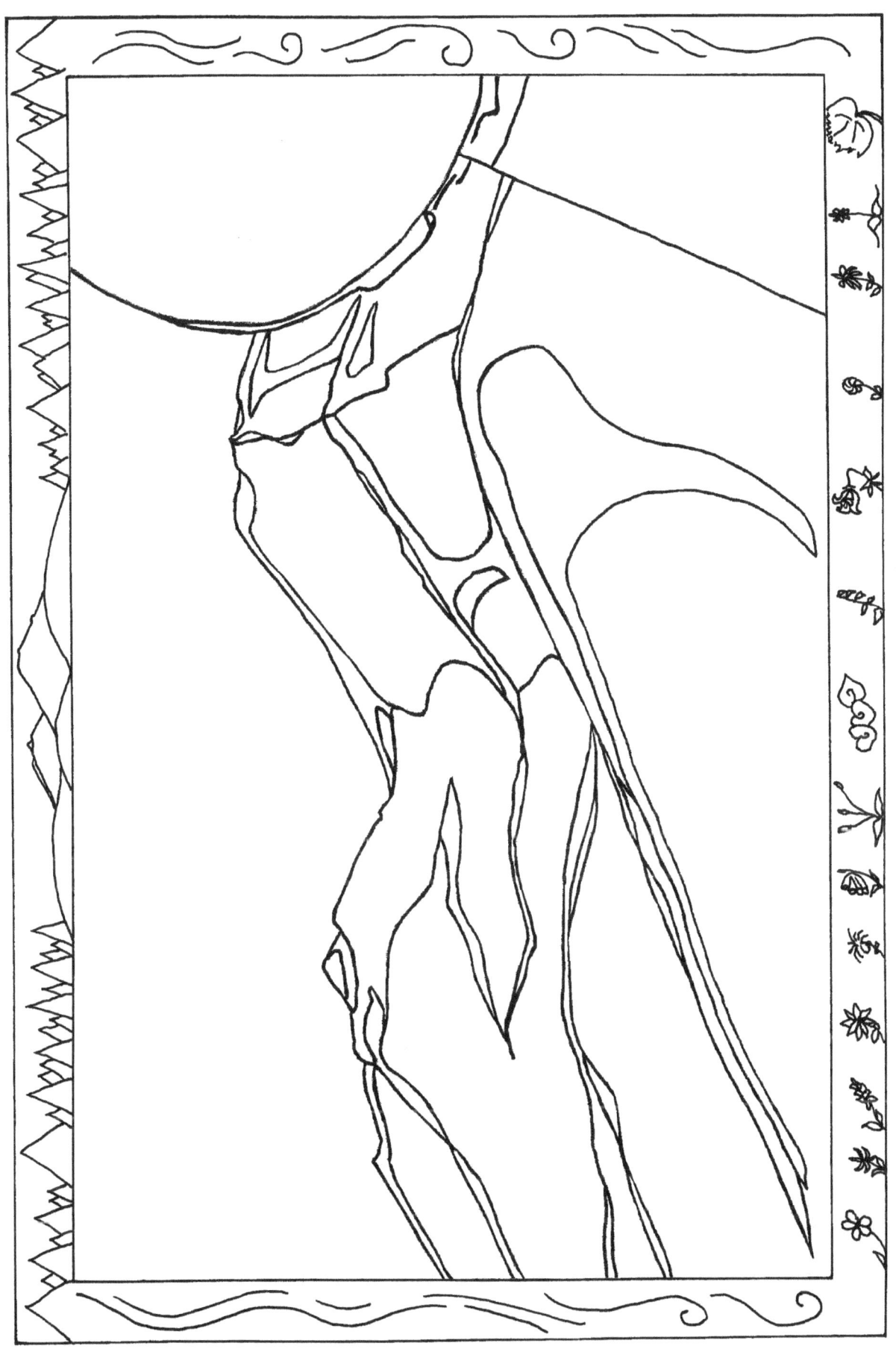

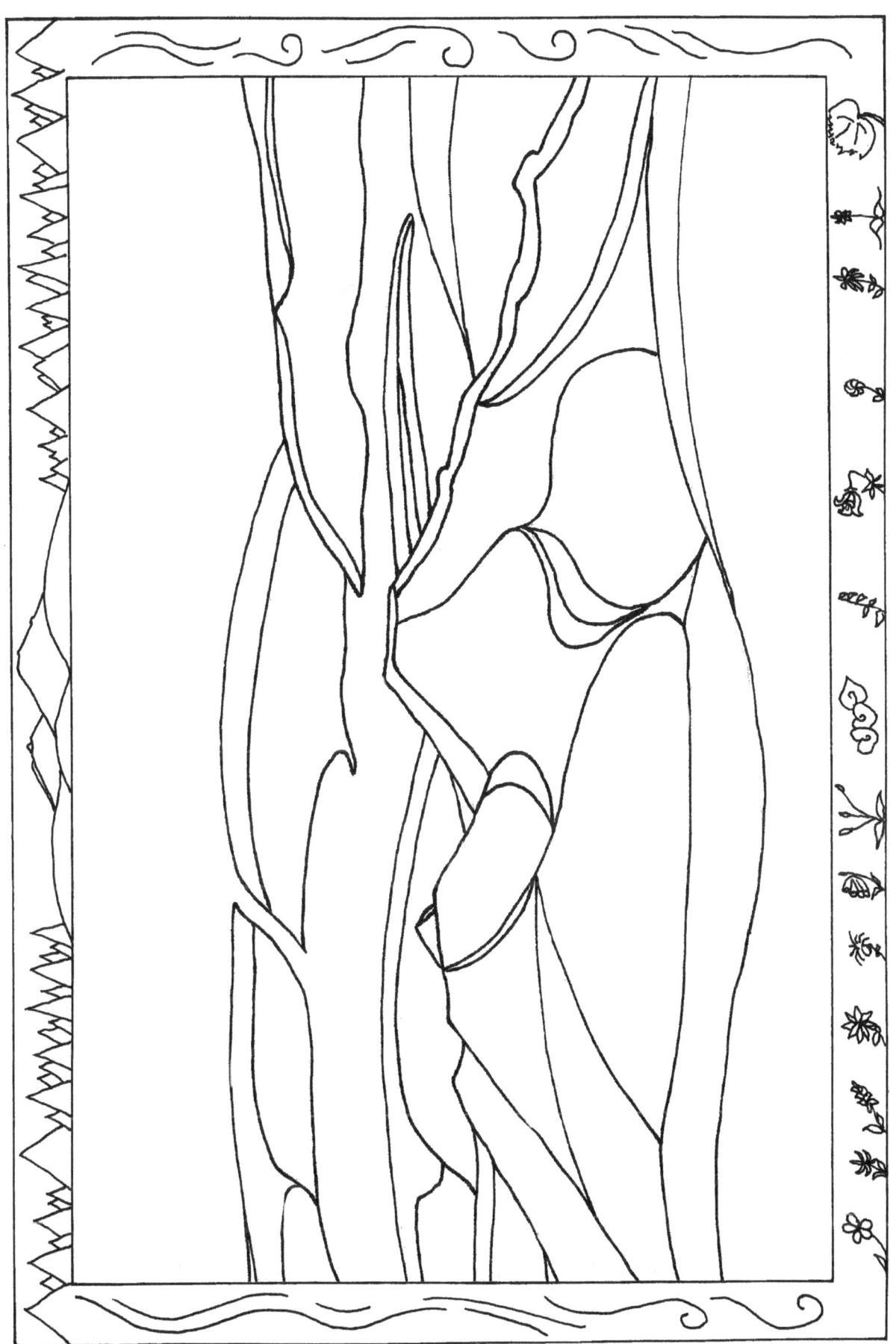

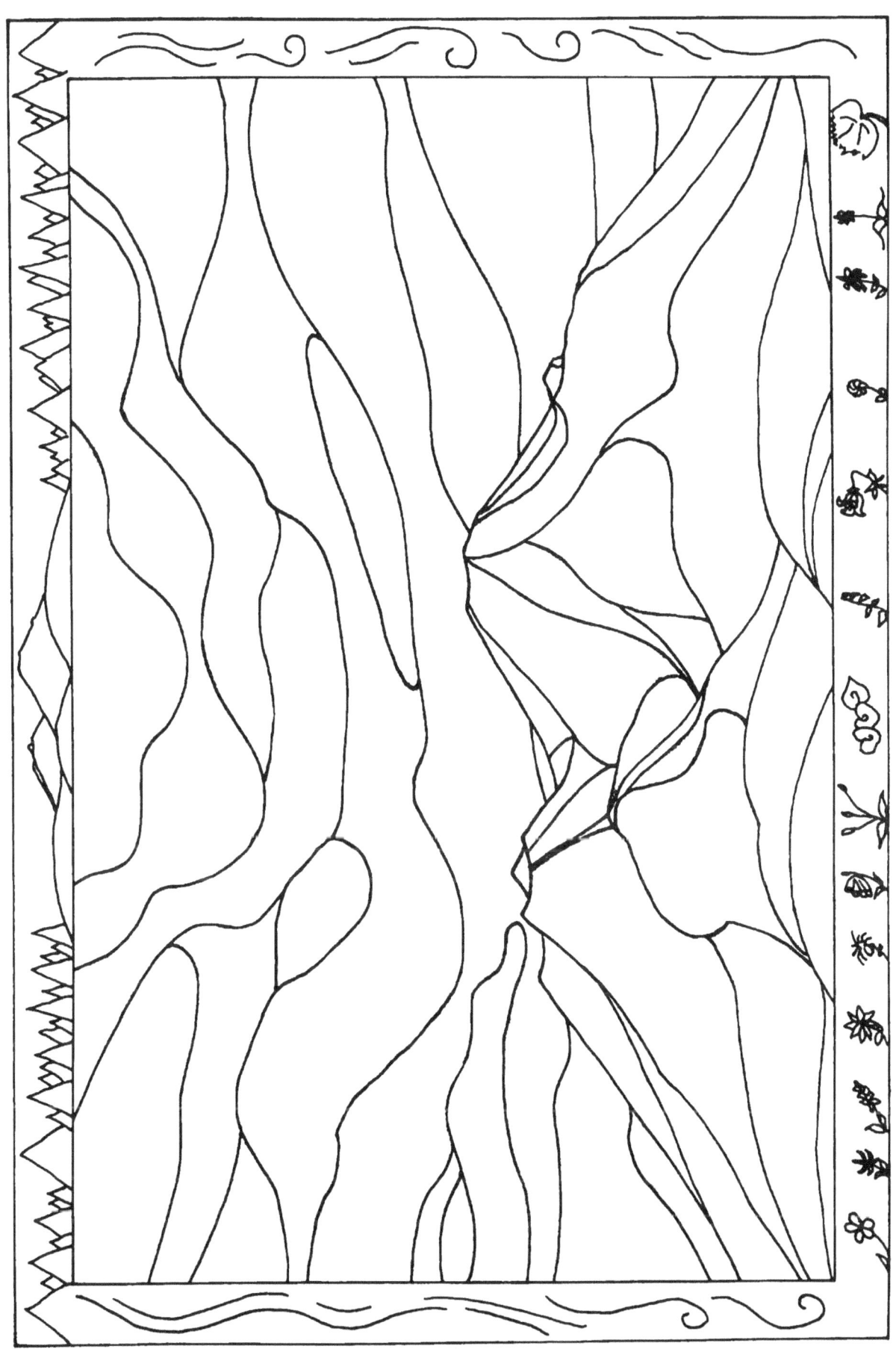

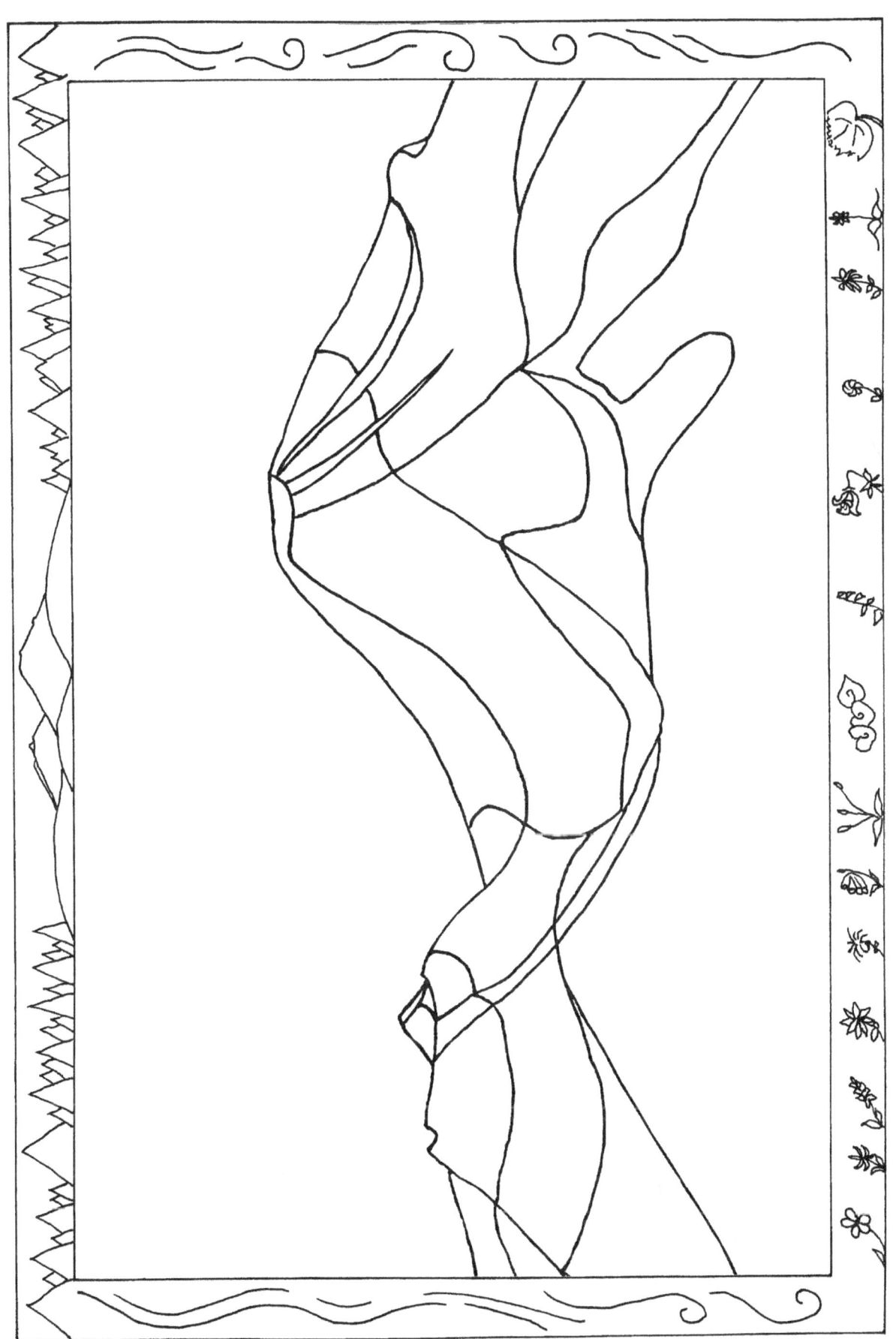

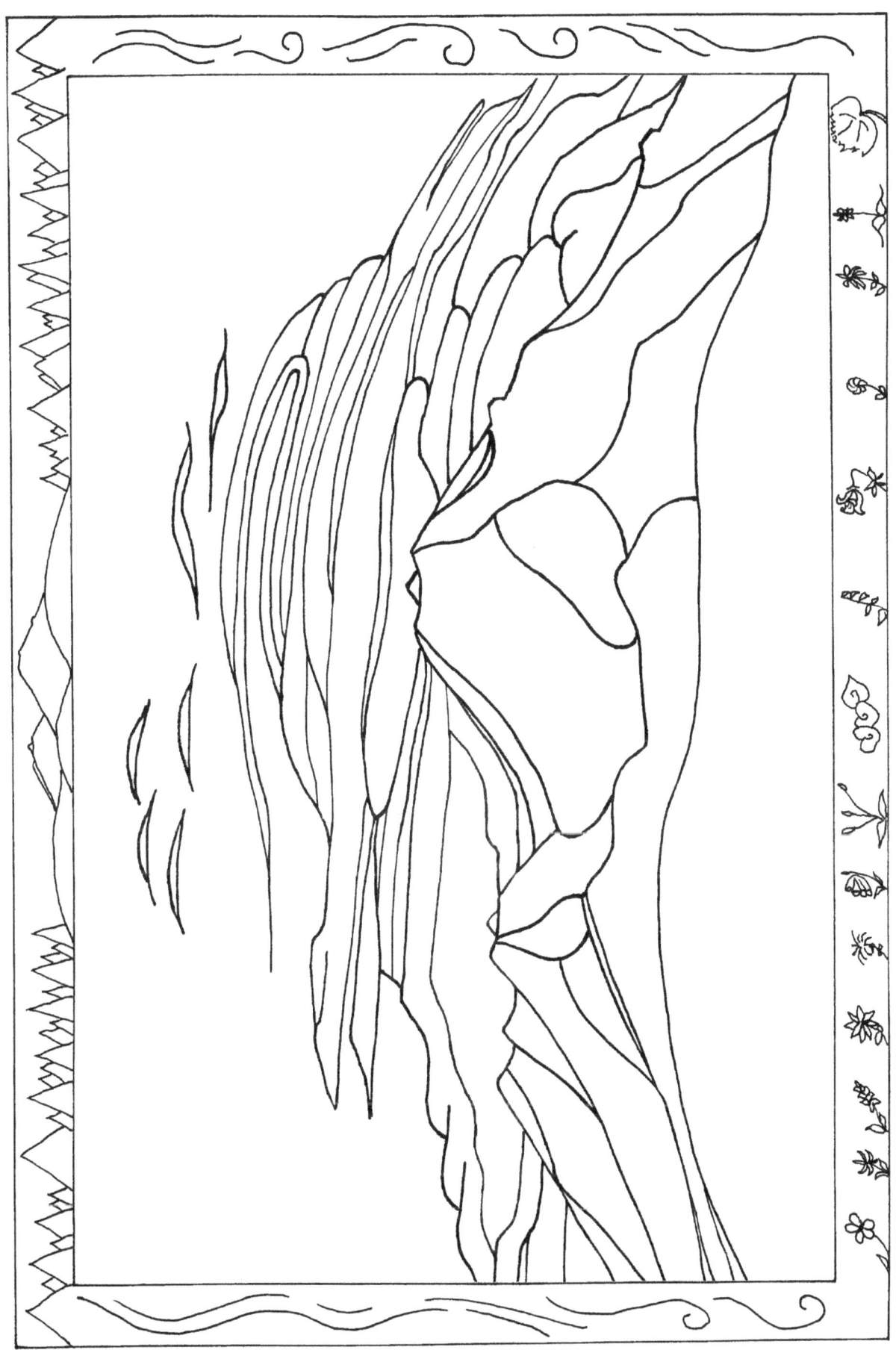

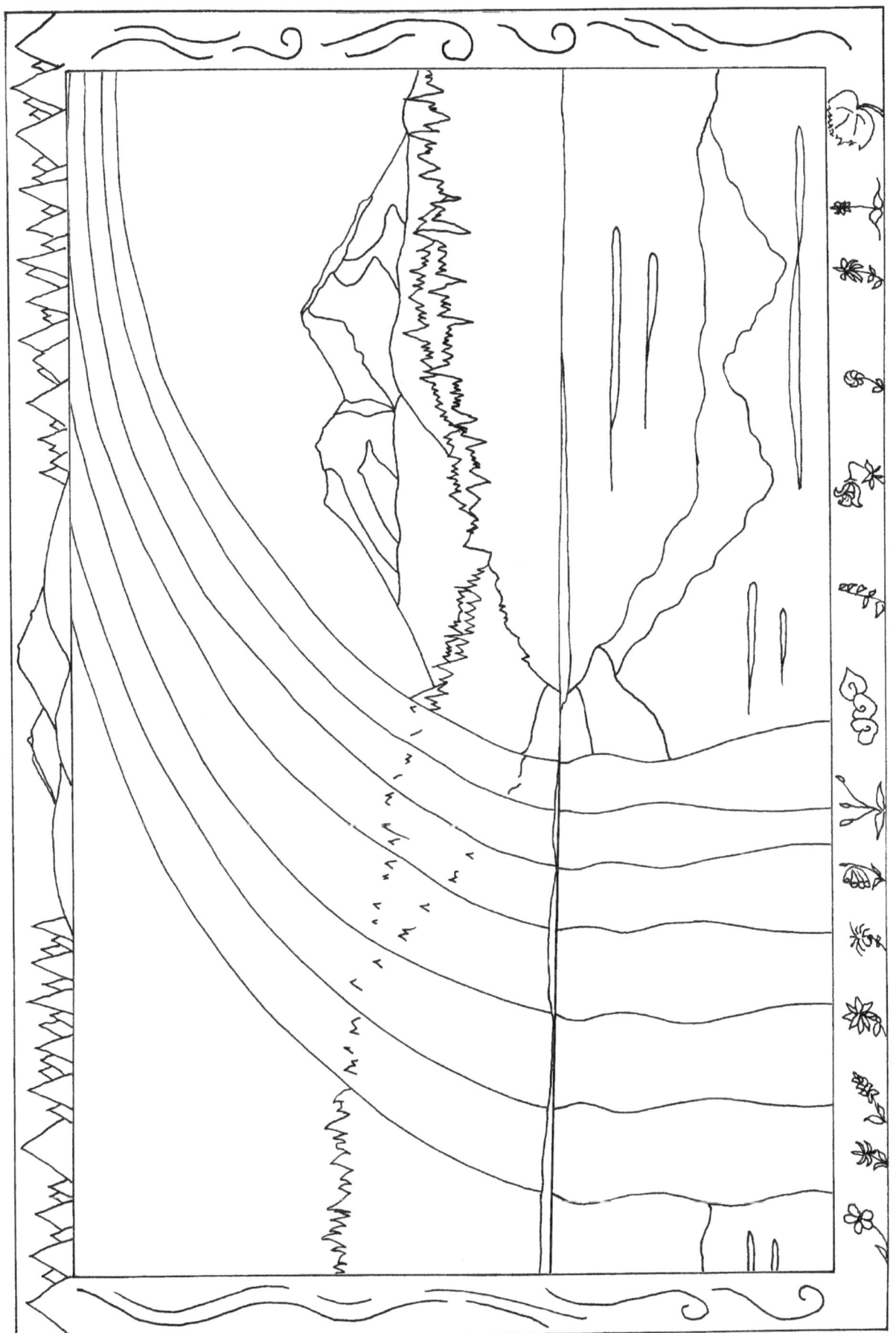

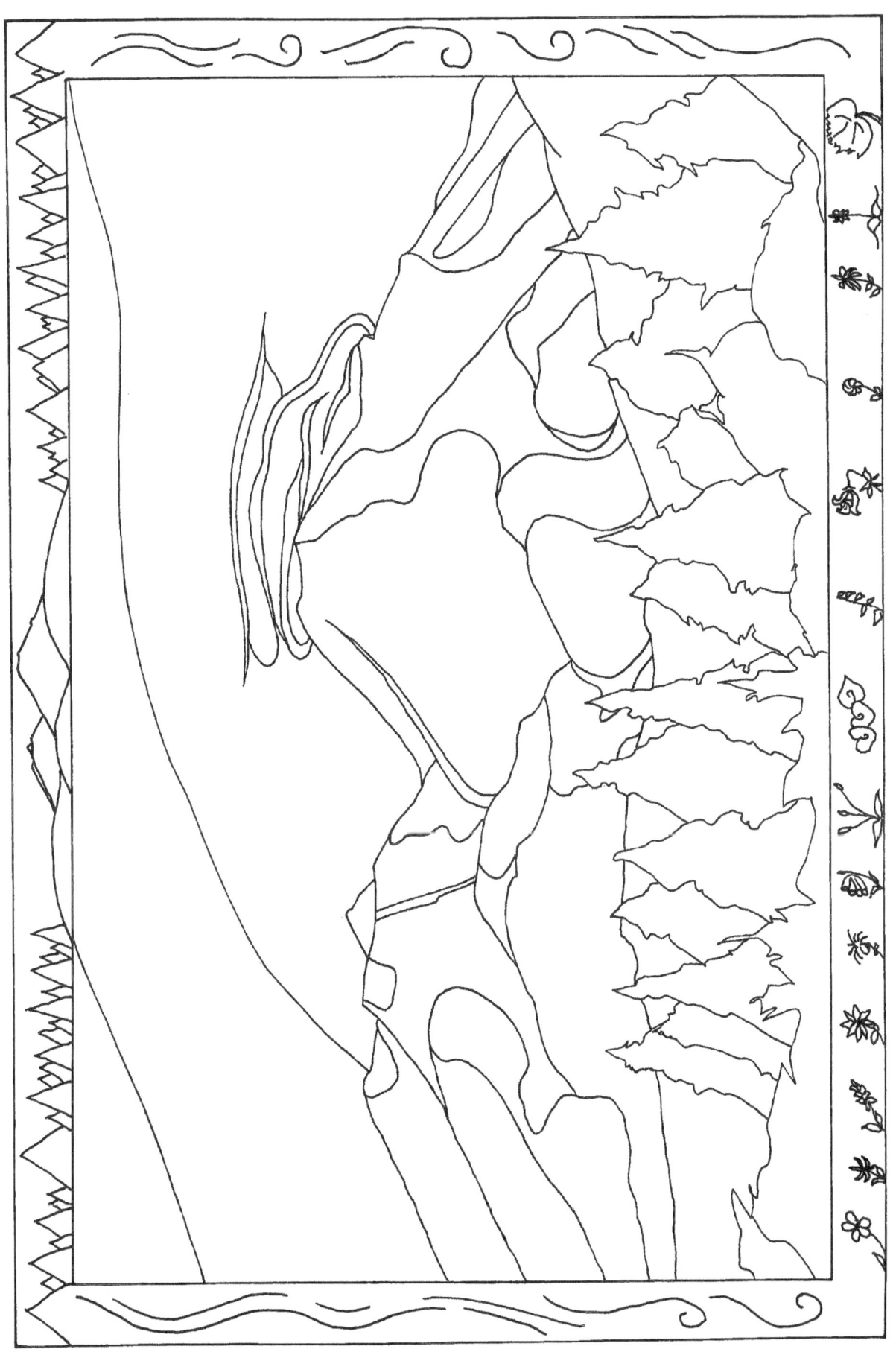

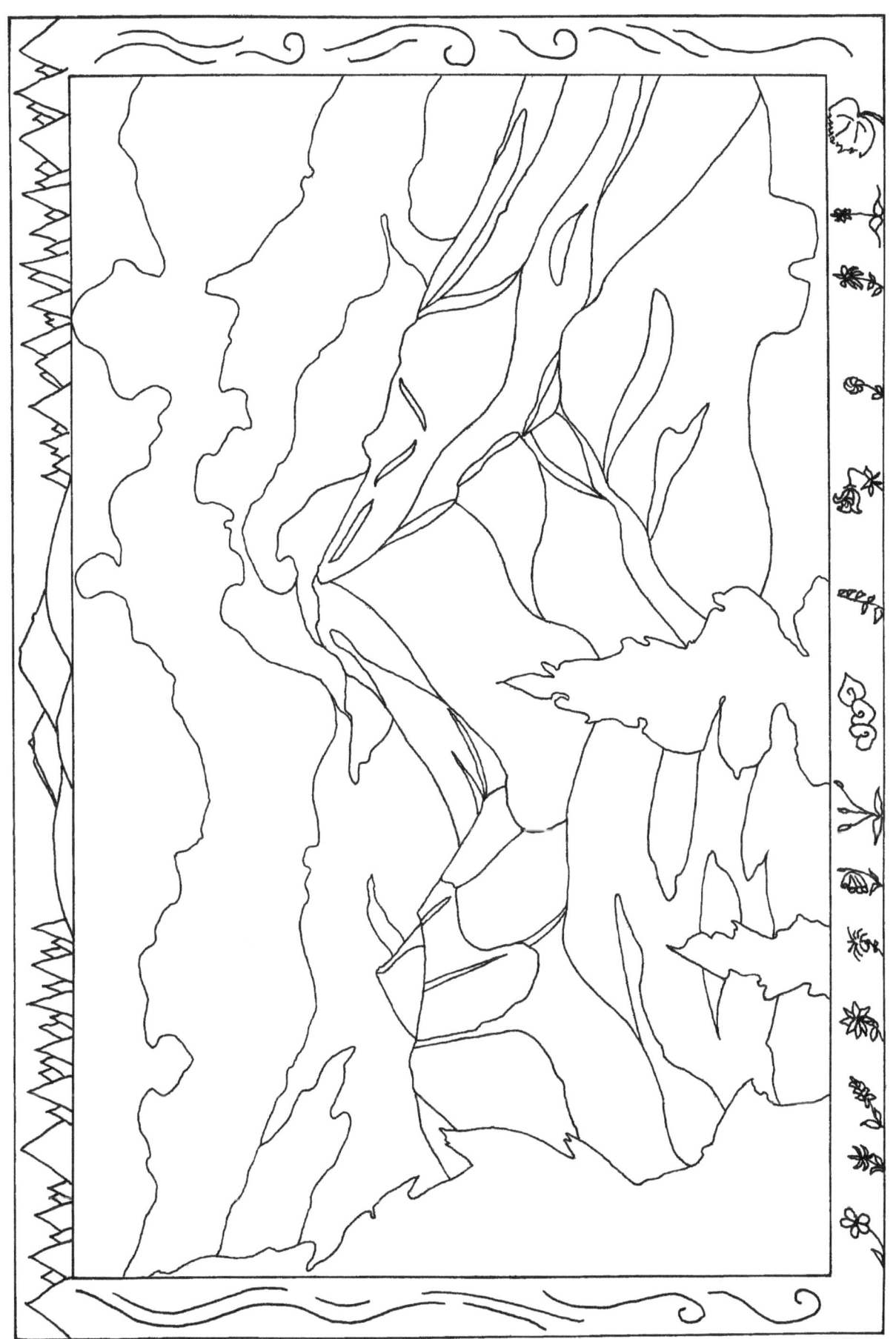

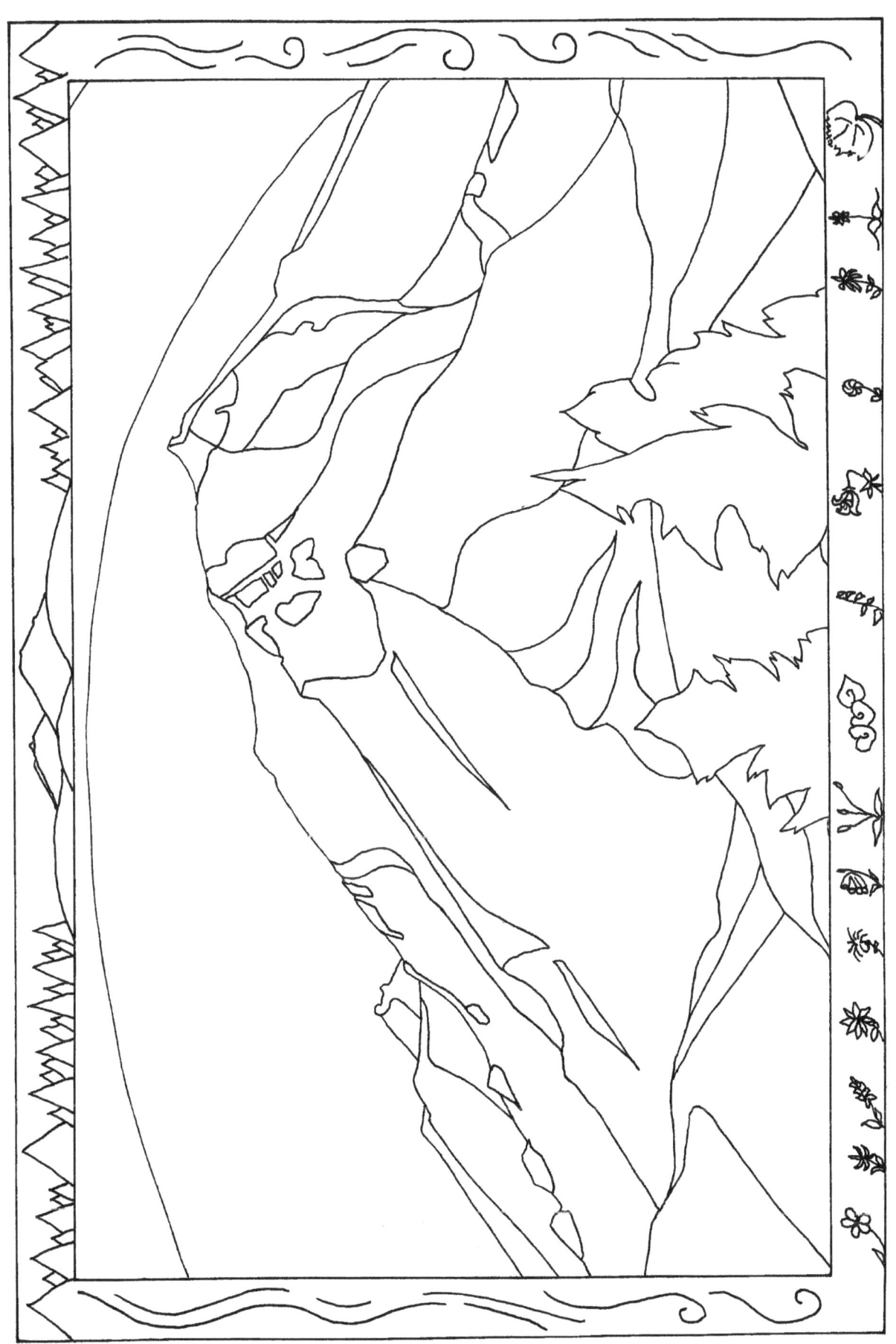

BLOTTER PAGE